All About
Water

Ann McCallum Staats, M.Ed.

Consultants

Dr. Aaron O'Dea
Staff Scientist
Smithsonian Tropical Research Institute

Cheryl Lane, M.Ed.
Seventh Grade Science Teacher
Chino Valley Unified School District

Michelle Wertman, M.S.Ed.
Literacy Specialist
New York City Public Schools

Publishing Credits

Rachelle Cracchiolo, M.S.Ed., *Publisher*
Emily R. Smith, M.A.Ed., *SVP of Content Development*
Véronique Bos, *VP of Creative*
Dani Neiley, *Editor*
Robin Erickson, *Senior Art Director*
Kevin Pham, *Senior Graphic Designer*

Smithsonian Enterprises

Avery Naughton, *Licensing Coordinator*
Paige Towler, *Editorial Lead*
Jill Corcoran, *Senior Director, Licensed Publishing*
Brigid Ferraro, *Vice President of New Business and Licensing*
Carol LeBlanc, *President*

Image Credits: p.12 Emily Stone/USAP; p.13 NASA;
all other images iStock and/or Shutterstock, or in the public domain

Library of Congress Cataloging in Publication Control Number: 2024033338

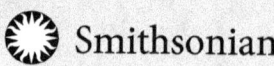

5482 Argosy Avenue
Huntington Beach, CA 92649
www.tcmpub.com
ISBN 979-8-7659-6874-1
© 2025 Teacher Created Materials, Inc.

Table of Contents

Water, Water, Everywhere 4

Small Wonder 6

Three States of Water 10

Flowing Places 16

The Power of Water 20

A Precious Resource 26

STEAM Challenge 28

Glossary 30

Index 31

Career Advice 32

Water, Water, Everywhere

Can you think of one thing that all humans, plants, and animals have in common? Here's a hint: all three need a substance that has no color, taste, or smell.

If you guessed *water*, you're right! Most organisms need water to survive. Water is the reason why life can exist on our planet. Many organisms would not be able to function without it.

Around 71 percent of Earth's surface is covered in water. Most of that is salt water, which is the water that makes up our oceans. But fresh water also exists across our planet. Glaciers, lakes, rivers, and more contain fresh water.

ocean

lake

river

glacier

Water is a unique substance in nature. It has special properties and behaviors. Water exists in three different states of matter: liquid, solid, and gas. A process called *the water cycle* explains how water moves around Earth. Water is the reason why we experience clouds, rain, snow, and fog. Water also plays a part in shaping landscapes through processes including **erosion**.

Water has countless uses around the world. Scientists have developed ways to turn fresh water into different kinds of drinking water. People use water to cook, clean, bathe, water their plants, and more. In places where fresh water is not readily available, people have special methods of collecting or purifying water. Let's dive in and learn all about water!

~56%	~59%	~59%	~60%	~60%	~75%
50+ years	19–50 years	12–18 years	1–12 years	0.6–1 years	0–0.6 years

The Stats

All living organisms are made up largely of water. Human babies are about 75 percent water. As they get older, the amount of water that makes up their bodies decreases. Adults are made up of about 55 to 65 percent water. Water is essential for human bodies to function.

MATHEMATICS

Small Wonder

By examining a single water molecule, we can understand what it is made of and why it acts the way it does. Every molecule of water is made up of two elements called *hydrogen* and *oxygen*. Two hydrogen atoms and one oxygen atom combine to form a water molecule. Have you ever seen the symbol H_2O? This is the chemical formula for water. It represents two hydrogen atoms and one oxygen atom.

Water molecules are incredibly small. In the tiniest drop of water, there are billions of water molecules. This is true for every type of water: fresh water, salt water, or **purified** water.

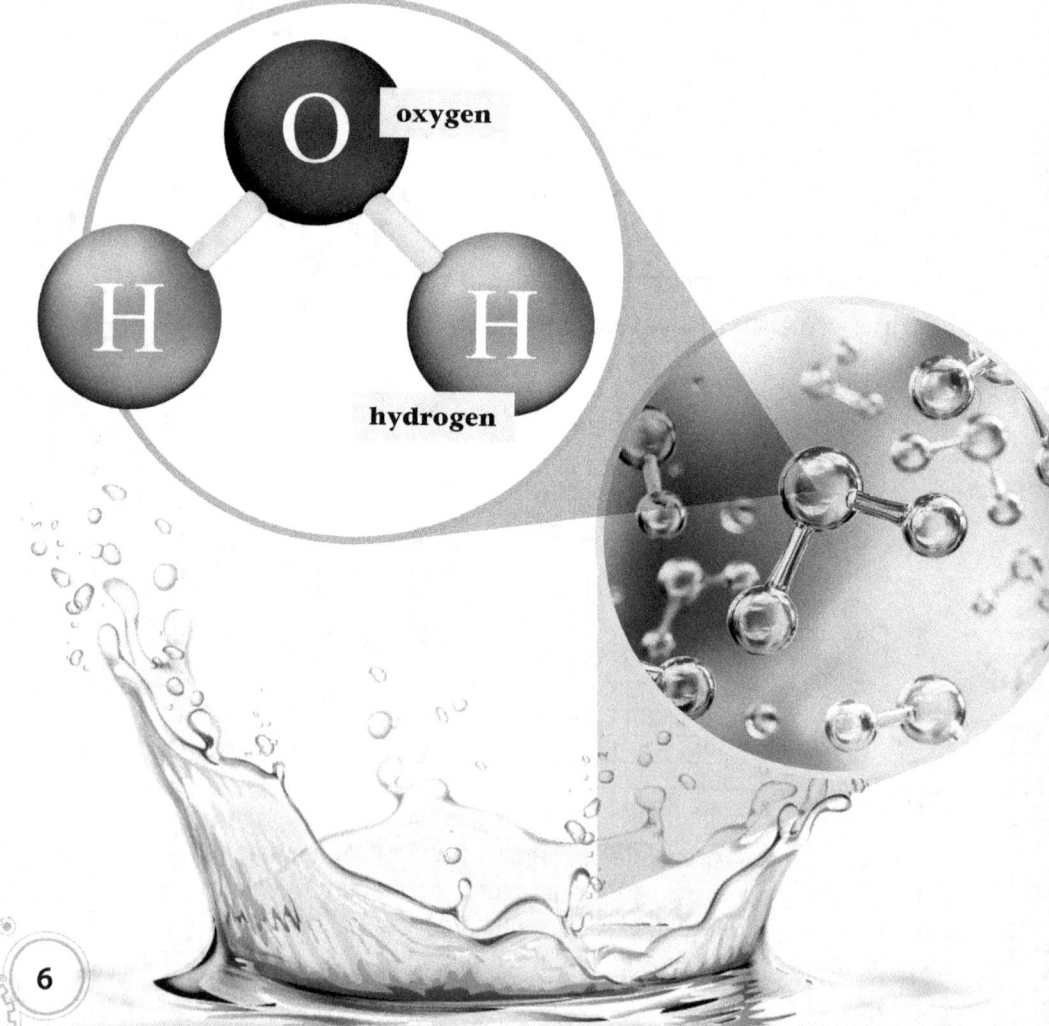

oxygen

hydrogen

Behavior

Particles inside the atoms of water molecules have electrical charges that affect how water behaves. The two hydrogen atoms have positive charges. The oxygen atom has a negative charge. Together, these charges act like a magnet. This makes water molecules cohesive, meaning they are attracted to one another. So, in large quantities, such as a bathtub, lake, or ocean, water functions as a whole. It moves together in large or small waves.

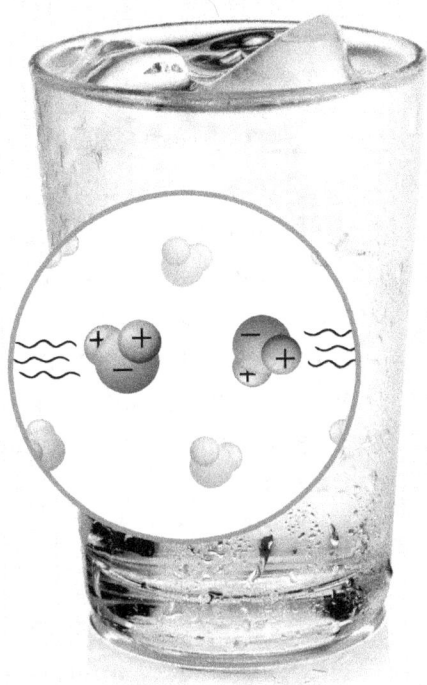

Water molecules are also adhesive. This means that they are drawn to different molecules. This is why water clings to some surfaces. For example, water can collect on the sides of drinking glasses.

Surface Tension

Water has a high surface tension, which means the surface of water is strong. When air is above the water's surface, water molecules only pull down and sideways. This creates resistance, which supports small objects that would usually sink. Thanks to surface tension, tiny insects can rest on top of water.

water strider

Taste and Smell

Pour yourself a glass of water, and take a sip. Do you taste anything? Then, take a whiff of it. Do you smell anything? If you have a glass of purified water, you won't be able to taste or smell anything. But if you have a glass of river water, ocean water, or pond water, that might be a different story. Some fresh water and ocean water sources may contain other substances. Sediment, plant matter, or **microorganisms** may be in these water sources. These substances can affect taste and smell. But in filtered water, all these substances are removed.

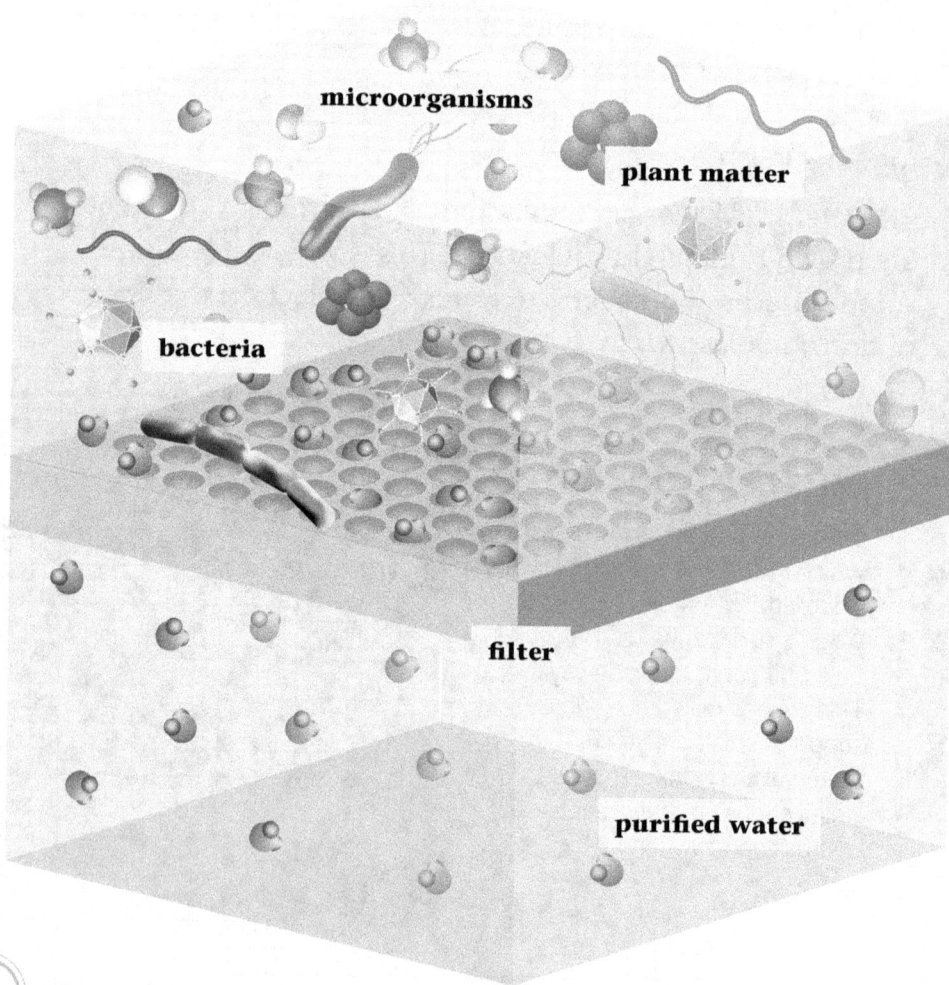

microorganisms

plant matter

bacteria

filter

purified water

Ponds are bodies of water that are smaller than lakes.

Solvent

Water is sometimes called the *universal solvent*. A solvent breaks down and dissolves other substances. Water has the unique property of being able to dissolve more substances than any other liquid on Earth. This is helpful for all life on Earth. Water can dissolve and transport chemicals, nutrients, and minerals that are necessary for survival. For example, in the human body, kidneys filter substances from recently eaten food and drinks. Water carries these waste products out of the body.

Not every substance mixes well with water. For example, oil does not combine with water. No matter how hard you shake or stir the mixture, the two substances will separate once you stop.

FUN FACT

Bubbly drinks, such as sodas, are created by adding carbon dioxide gas to water. When the gas is added to water, it creates tiny bubbles. These bubbles fizz and rise to the surface of the drink. They give drinks like sodas their sharp, bubbly taste.

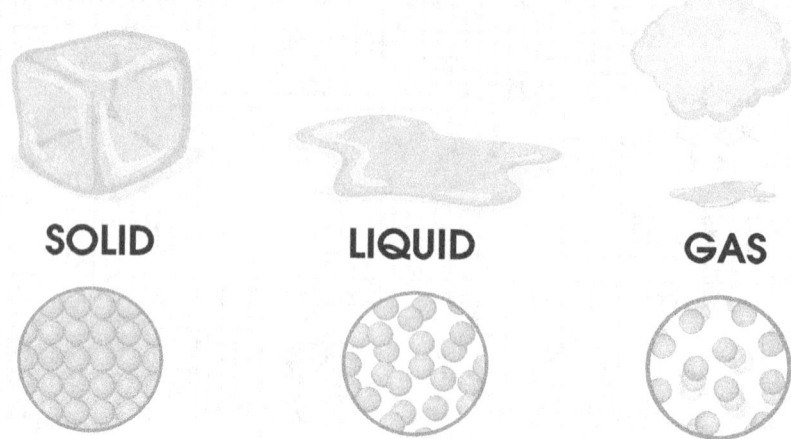

SOLID   **LIQUID**   **GAS**

Three States of Water

All matter can exist in four different states: solid, liquid, gas, or **plasma**. Water exists in three of these states. It is the only known substance that occurs in nature as a solid, liquid, and gas. Plus, water can change between these states while keeping its same properties. These are physical changes, and they can be reversed. Adding or removing heat causes liquid water to transform into a gas or a solid. And when water is in these three states, it looks and behaves differently.

Clouds form when liquid water **evaporates** into a gas.

Liquid State

Liquid water covers 71 percent of Earth's surface. This includes salt water and fresh water, which we'll explore in depth in the next chapter. Rain comes from clouds as liquid water. Of the three states, liquid water is the most **dense**. That's because the molecules in liquid water are close together.

Water molecules are always vibrating. And the faster the molecules move, the warmer they are. Around the world, liquid water exists at a range of temperatures. Water is in a liquid state above 0 °C to 100 °C (32 °F to 212 °F). When the temperature of water goes below 0 °C (32 °F), it freezes into ice. It changes from a liquid to a solid state. When the temperature of water goes above 100 °C (212 °F), it begins to boil. This makes it change from a liquid state to a gas state.

Solid State

When liquid water freezes, the position of the water molecules changes. The molecules arrange themselves into a crystal pattern with plenty of space in between. This structure makes ice less dense than liquid water. Because ice is less dense than liquid water, it will form on top of the water. Even in winter, when many bodies of water freeze, liquid water still exists below the ice. Fish and other underwater creatures survive there until spring.

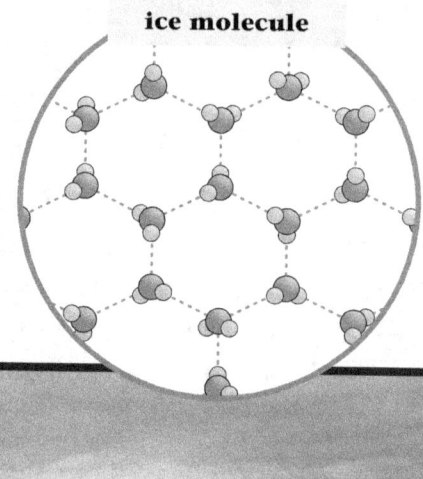

water molecule

ice molecule

In Antarctica, emperor penguins hunt for fish, krill, and squid under the ice.

Grey Glacier in Patagonia, Chile

On Earth, solid water includes snow, **hail**, and ice, which also forms as glaciers and icebergs. The largest mass of ice on Earth is found in Antarctica. It is a type of glacier called an *ice sheet* that is made up of frozen fresh water. It has an area of about 14 million square kilometers (5.4 million square miles). Icebergs are also made of frozen fresh water. They form by separating from glaciers. Icebergs are like ice cubes in oceans. They float because the density of the ice is less than the density of the water.

Some places on Earth have snow on the ground nearly year-round. This occurs in high-altitude regions, such as the Andes Mountains or Rocky Mountains. However, snow and ice can transform from a solid state back to a liquid state by melting. **Thermal energy**, such as from the sun, makes snow and ice melt.

FUN FACT

Icebergs can range in size from small to large. In 2000, an iceberg that was nearly the size of the state of Connecticut appeared in the ocean. It broke off from the Ross Ice Shelf in Antarctica. Over time, this iceberg broke up into smaller icebergs.

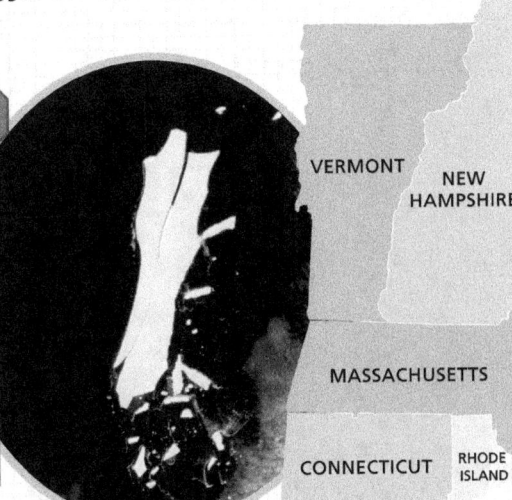

VERMONT

NEW HAMPSHIRE

MASSACHUSETTS

CONNECTICUT   RHODE ISLAND

Gas State

Thermal energy causes water to evaporate into a gas or vapor. Think of boiling a pot of water on the stove. When it begins to boil, you will see steam rising from the pot. That's water in a gas state.

On Earth, heat from the sun causes water to evaporate. The air holds on to this moisture. The amount of water vapor in the air is called *humidity*. Some parts of the world experience high humidity. The air may feel thick and steamy, especially when it's hot.

As water evaporates, it turns into invisible water vapor.

Grand Prismatic Spring is Yellowstone National Park's largest hot spring.

Bubbling, boiling, steaming water occurs naturally on Earth. It is called *geothermal water*. This type of water is heated under Earth's surface. It can form natural hot springs, which are pleasantly warm pools of water. But some geothermal waters form geysers and fumaroles, which can be dangerous. Geysers spew hot water and steam from vents in the ground. For example, Old Faithful is a well-known geyser in Yellowstone National Park. Fumaroles release steam and volcanic gases from the ground. Both of these features are found near volcanic activity.

Sometimes, the amount of water vapor in the air reaches a **saturation** point. The vapor begins to condense, or turn back into a liquid, on particles of dust found in the air. When enough vapor condenses, it causes fog or clouds to form. When the liquid droplets in clouds become too heavy, they fall back to Earth as rain.

FUN FACT

Fog commonly occurs in valleys or near bodies of water. It forms when the air is cool and humid. When the air starts to warm up again, fog begins to evaporate.

Flowing Places

The two main types of water on Earth are fresh water and salt water. These types of water have distinct features and uses. These sources are found in different places on our planet.

Fresh Water

Human bodies have veins that carry blood throughout our systems. Likewise, rivers carry fresh water across the continents on Earth. These bodies of water start on high ground at sources called *headwaters*. There, rain, melting snow, or water from within Earth collects and flows together. This water joins other bodies of water, such as rivers. Rivers may branch off to form smaller streams, creeks, or **tributaries**. Rivers can flow uphill, downhill, or follow the path of least resistance. Eventually, rivers will reach the lowest point of the land and end. Then, they empty into larger bodies of water, such as oceans or lakes. Areas where rivers meet larger bodies of water are called *estuaries*.

Nanaimo River Estuary in Canada

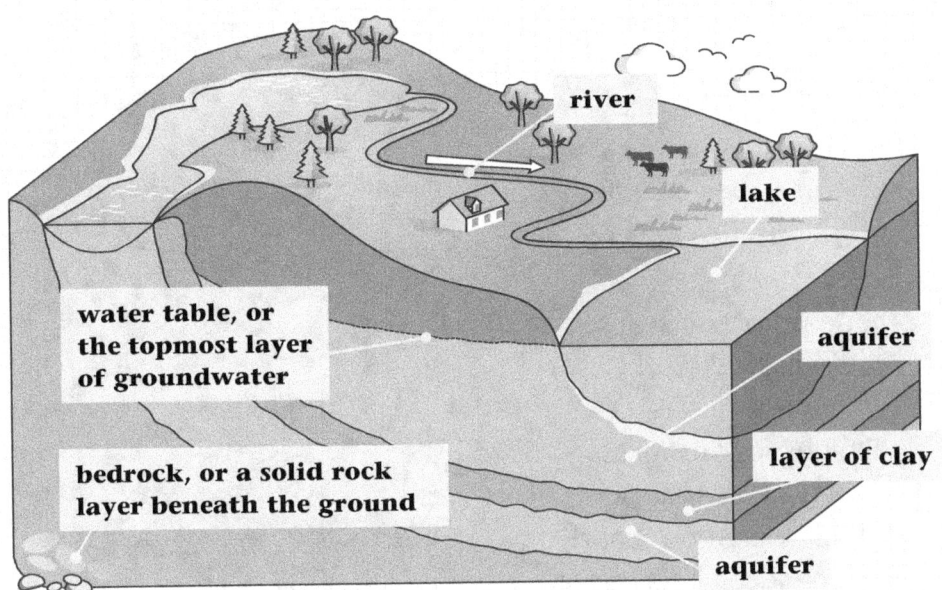

river

lake

water table, or the topmost layer of groundwater

aquifer

layer of clay

bedrock, or a solid rock layer beneath the ground

aquifer

As fresh water flows across the ground, some of it seeps into the soil and becomes groundwater. This is water that exists beneath the ground in spaces between soil, sand, and rock in layers called *aquifers*. Plants rely on groundwater to survive.

Other sources of fresh water exist on Earth, too. Some lakes were formed by glaciers melting into liquid water. Humans have created lakes by digging in the ground or using dams to reroute water from rivers. Ponds, which are smaller bodies of fresh water, can be created in these same ways.

ENGINEERING

Underground Systems

In many cities and towns, large systems of drains and pipes are built underground. These systems are used to carry rainwater away from streets. These pipes may lead to rivers or oceans. Engineers design these complex systems to be as efficient as possible.

Salt Water

The majority of water found on Earth is salt water. That's because Earth's oceans are made up of salt water. Different bodies of water have different salinities, or amounts of salt in them. Oceans contain between 3 and 5 percent salt. A special type of water called *brine water* contains even more salt. The Dead Sea, which borders Jordan and Israel, is 34 percent salt. The Great Salt Lake in Utah varies between 5 to 27 percent salt. The salinity varies due to the height, or level, of the water.

the Dead Sea

Sometimes, salt water mixes with fresh water, creating brackish water. This type of water can occur in estuaries. Brackish water has a salinity that is between fresh water and salt water.

Mangrove forests are common in areas where fresh water and salt water meet.

For humans and certain types of plants and animals, drinking salt water is dangerous. These organisms cannot process the high amount of salt. They would eventually die of **dehydration**. However, plenty of wildlife thrives in salt water. Scientists estimate they have identified over 215,000 different marine species, from the tiniest brine shrimp to the largest blue whales. Some scientists estimate there are another two million species yet to be discovered!

Although the oceans cover most of our planet, scientists estimate that only five percent have been explored. High **water pressure** makes it difficult to explore ocean depths.

brine shrimp

Recreational scuba divers can only dive to 40 meters (130 feet) below the water's surface for safety reasons.

The Power of Water

On our planet, water is power. It is a resource, a force, and a necessity. In nature, water cycles through its three states of matter as a **renewable resource**. Excess water creates extreme storms and can reshape landscapes over time. But some people are able to use the power of water in useful and surprising ways.

The Water Cycle

The amount of water on Earth has remained unchanged throughout time. A nonstop process called *the water cycle* moves water on Earth.

In high regions of the world, melting snow and ice flow down into larger rivers. Heat from the sun causes water in rivers, oceans, lakes, and more to undergo evaporation. In this process, water molecules rise into the atmosphere as water vapor. The vapor rises more and mixes with cooler air. During condensation, the vapor transforms back into liquid droplets. These droplets take the form of clouds. As clouds build and become too heavy with water droplets, **precipitation** falls back to the ground for collection. Then, the whole cycle starts over!

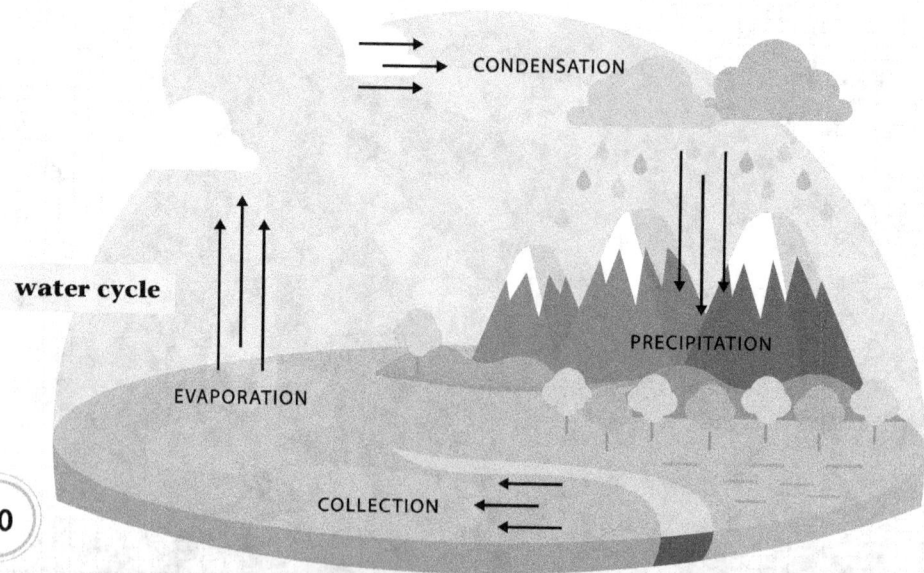

water cycle

CONDENSATION

PRECIPITATION

EVAPORATION

COLLECTION

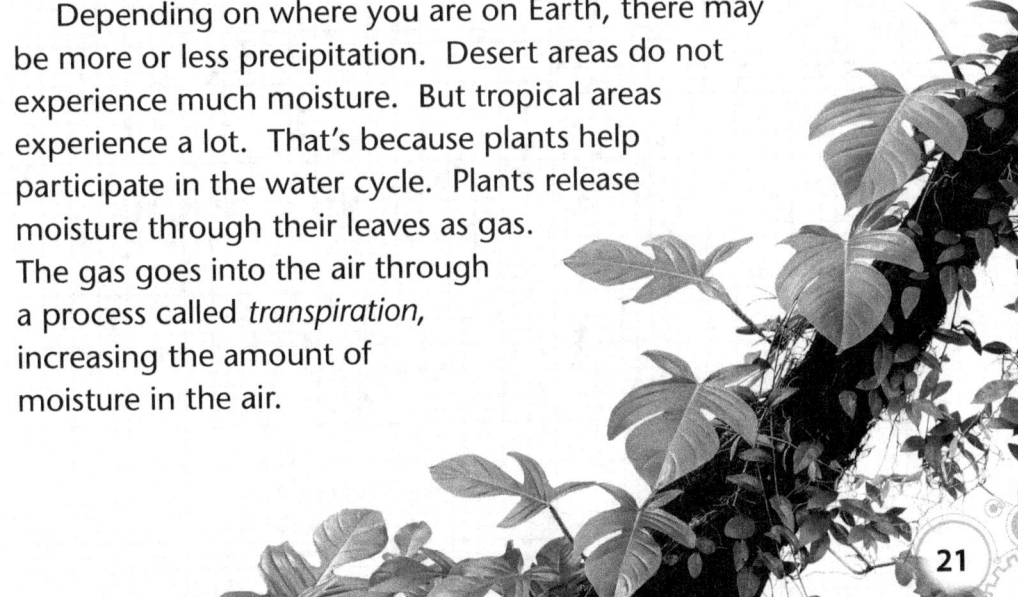

The Atacama Desert in Chile is one of the driest places in the world.

Depending on where you are on Earth, there may be more or less precipitation. Desert areas do not experience much moisture. But tropical areas experience a lot. That's because plants help participate in the water cycle. Plants release moisture through their leaves as gas. The gas goes into the air through a process called *transpiration*, increasing the amount of moisture in the air.

Extreme Events

Certain factors, such as temperature and wind, can result in powerful water events. One example is a hurricane. This is a strong storm that forms over oceans. First, ocean water evaporates into clouds. As more moisture is picked up, heavy rain occurs. Forceful winds begin to mix with the heavy rain, making the storm grow stronger. If a hurricane moves over land, it quickly becomes destructive and can cause heavy damage.

Other extreme events include hail and flooding. Hail occurs when droplets of water in clouds freeze into solid pieces and fall to the ground. Large pieces of hail are especially dangerous and can damage buildings. Flooding occurs when the ground becomes saturated with water and can't absorb any more liquid. These extreme events negatively affect people, animals, and plants.

pieces of hail

People on bike taxis drive through a flooded street in Bangladesh.

The Colorado River wore away the rock walls of the Grand Canyon.

Over Time

Water has the power to make many transformations to landscapes. Over long periods, water changes Earth's surface. Water is a key part of erosion, which is the wearing away of materials on Earth over time. In the Grand Canyon in Arizona, water wore away large parts of the rocky ground. Its power left behind a gaping canyon deep in the ground. Another example of erosion can be seen in the **limestone** islands of Ha Long Bay, Vietnam. Water flooded and wore away the limestone mountains over thousands of years. This left a few tall mountains standing in a large body of water.

Addressing a Lack of Water

Although water is a renewable resource, clean and fresh water is not always available to people. Around the world, four billion people experience **water scarcity** for at least

rain barrel

one month every year. Scarcity can be caused by many different reasons, such as **droughts** or pollution. This lack of access to clean water makes life very difficult.

To fight this problem, humans have developed new ways to access water. For example, some people use rain barrels to collect rainwater. These huge barrels catch water falling from the sky, and people filter the water for their own use. Also, scientists have created a process called *cloud seeding*. They add tiny ice-like particles to clouds to help kickstart the formation of rain. Another example is a process called *desalination*. Salt water is put through a complex system of filters to remove all the salt, creating drinkable water. However, this method is extremely expensive, and it does not create a large amount of fresh water.

DESALINATION

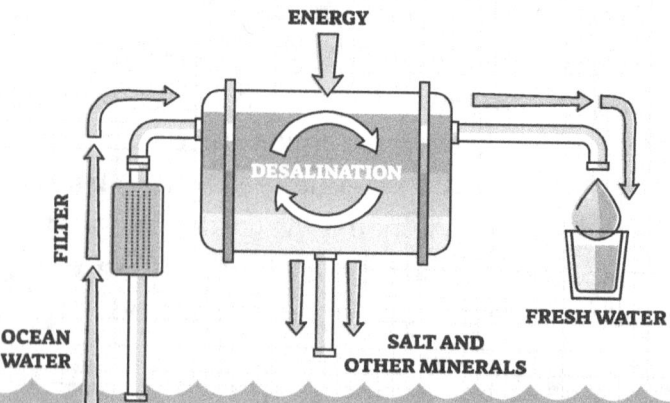

ENERGY

FILTER

DESALINATION

FRESH WATER

OCEAN WATER

SALT AND OTHER MINERALS

Water conservation is one more solution that can help in situations where water is scarce. Conservation involves the careful management and protection of a resource. Whenever possible, people should use water efficiently. To avoid waste, they should only use the amount of water that they need. For example, while washing dishes, turning off the faucet instead of leaving it running is one easy way to conserve water.

Drought-tolerant plants aid in water conservation because they can handle periods of dryness.

Water as Power

Special technology allows people to capture water's force. Using specially made dams and **generators**, the energy from moving water can be captured. The energy can be converted into hydroelectricity. This is a clean form of energy, meaning it does not cause pollution like the burning of coal or gas. Six percent of electricity in the United States comes from water!

A Precious Resource

If you cup some water in your hand, it may seem light and insubstantial. But this liquid is a powerful and precious resource. Water flows through many places across our planet, from the highest peaks to the deepest depths of the oceans. It can take the form of the largest glaciers or the tiniest drops of rain. Over millions of years, water has shaped our landscape. Deep valleys and steep canyons have their impressive appearances thanks to water. Plus, the water cycle ensures that fresh and salt water is continually changing around the globe. Whether water is in a liquid, solid, or gas state, it has an impact on Earth.

ARTS

Fun with Water

Some people seek out water in its various states for recreational fun. Swimming, kayaking, and scuba diving are popular activities in bodies of water. Snow sports, such as snowboarding and skiing, take place on snow-covered mountains. Saunas and spas make use of water vapor as steam. All over the world, people turn the world's most powerful resource into powerful fun!

Water holes are important to the survival of many African animals.

Water plays a role in the survival of every living thing. People use water for drinking, washing, and cooking. They can also use water to help grow crops or generate energy. Without water, plants cannot grow. Animals need water to survive in their environments. Scientists continue to work to find new ways to recycle and conserve water. They want to make sure there is enough clean water available now and in the future.

Rice plants receive water that is pumped from the ground.

An oasis is an area in a desert where water can be found.

STEAM CHALLENGE

Define the Problem

In our global economy, about one trillion dollars' worth of food is wasted annually. Much of this loss is caused by food spoiling or melting during transportation. Food scientists want to develop more efficient, temperature-controlled storage methods. Your task is to develop a model food storage unit. It should allow frozen items to maintain a frozen state, preventing spoilage or melting.

Constraints: You may only use the materials that are provided to you.

Criteria: Your model food storage unit must be able to open and close for convenience. It must be no larger than 0.6 meters (2 feet) wide and tall. Ice cubes must stay frozen for an extended period inside the unit while it is placed under a heat lamp. You must also have a water collection cup under the ice compartment to collect and measure any runoff.

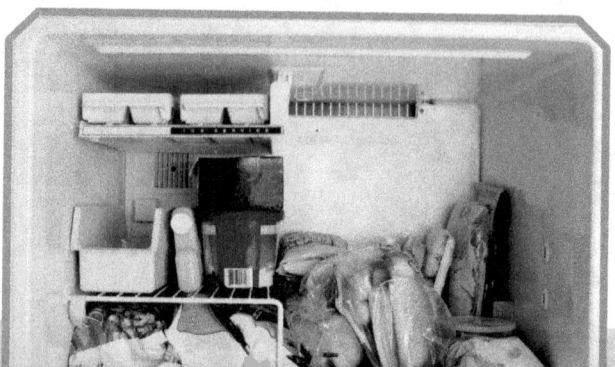

Research and Brainstorm

What is thermal energy? How does thermal energy affect the states of matter? How might thermal energy affect the success rate of food transportation on a global level?

Design and Build

Sketch a design for your model food storage unit. Label the materials you will use to reduce thermal energy transfer. Share your ideas with your small group, and together, develop a final design. Work together to build your model.

Test and Improve

Turn on your group's heat lamp, and open your model food storage unit. Place five ice cubes inside, above the water collection cup. Move your model directly under the heat lamp, and set a five-minute timer. After five minutes, open your unit and empty any water into the collection cup for measurement. Did your model prevent thermal energy transfer to the ice inside? How might you adjust your model to help maintain a frozen state? Make changes to your design and rebuild as necessary.

Reflect and Share

What part of this challenge was the most difficult? Where did your team find success? Were you able to resolve conflicts collaboratively? What external factors can make food preservation and transportation a challenge?

Glossary

dehydration—a harmful reduction in the amount of water in the body

dense—closely compacted; having a high mass per unit volume

droughts—long periods of dry weather with no precipitation

erosion—the wearing away of earth materials by water or wind

evaporates—turns from liquid into vapor

generators—machines that convert mechanical energy into electrical energy

hail—pellets of frozen rain that fall from clouds

limestone—a type of hard sedimentary rock that is often used as building material or in cement

microorganisms—organisms that are microscopic in size

particles—any basic units of matter and energy, such as molecules, atoms, protons, electrons, or photons

plasma—a state of matter that consists of charged particles in any combination of ions or electrons

precipitation—the amount of water that falls to Earth as hail, mist, rain, sleet, or snow

purified—made pure and clean

renewable resource—natural resource that is replenished naturally and won't run out

saturation—a state where the maximum amount of a substance has been absorbed or mixed in

thermal energy—energy in the form of heat

tributaries—streams that flow into larger streams or lakes

water pressure—the weight of water pressing down on an object due to gravity

water scarcity—a lack of fresh water resources to meet demand

Index

Antarctica, 12–13

conservation, 25

desalination, 24

erosion, 5, 23

flooding, 22

fresh water, 4–6, 8, 11, 13, 16–18, 24

geothermal water, 15

Grand Canyon, 23

groundwater, 17

Ha Long Bay, 23

hail, 13, 22

humidity, 14

hurricanes, 22

hydroelectricity, 25

icebergs, 13

lakes, 4, 9, 16–17, 20

properties of water, 5, 10

    behavior, 5, 7

    smell, 4, 8

    solvent, 9

    taste, 4, 8–9

rain, 5, 11, 15–17, 22, 24, 26

rivers, 4, 16–17, 20

salt water, 4, 6, 11, 16, 18–19, 24, 26

saturation, 15

snow, 5, 13, 16, 20, 26

states of water, 10

    gas, 5, 9–11, 14–15, 21, 25–26

    liquid, 5, 9–13, 15, 17, 20, 22, 26

    solid, 5, 9–13, 17, 22, 26

surface tension, 7

thermal energy, 13–14

water cycle, 5, 20–21, 26

water molecules, 6–7, 11–12, 20

water scarcity, 24

CAREER ADVICE
from Smithsonian

Do you want to work with water?

Here are some tips to keep in mind for the future.

"Start exploring life in your area, whether it's a local pond, a woodland, or the nearest coastline. Participate in local clean-up projects to learn about the oceans firsthand."

– Dr. Aaron O'Dea, Staff Scientist, Smithsonian Tropical Research Institute

"A great way to learn is outside the classroom! Learn about the water cycle–it's the journey water takes to reach your tap. Visit aquariums and marine parks to see marine biology in action."

– Dr. Erin Dillon, Postdoctoral Researcher, Smithsonian Tropical Research Institute

www.ingramcontent.com/pod-product-compliance
Lightning Source LLC
Chambersburg PA
CBHW06014415062626
46550CB00014B/1332